Rick and Morty™

MAD LIBS®

JOKE BOOK

by Brandon T. Snider

Mad Libs
An Imprint of Penguin Random House

MAD LIBS
Penguin Young Readers Group
An Imprint of Penguin Random House LLC

Concept created by Roger Price & Leonard Stern

[adult swim]

Published by Mad Libs,
an imprint of Penguin Random House LLC,
345 Hudson Street, New York, New York 10014.
Printed in the USA.

ISBN 9781524790738
1 3 5 7 9 10 8 6 4 2

MAD LIBS®

INSTRUCTIONS

MAD LIBS® is a game for people who don't like games! It can be played by one, two, three, four, or forty.

• RIDICULOUSLY SIMPLE DIRECTIONS

In this tablet you will find jokes containing blank spaces where words are left out. One player, the READER, selects a joke. The READER does not tell anyone what the joke is about. Instead, he/she asks the other players, the WRITERS, to give him/her words. These words are used to fill in the blank spaces in the joke.

• TO PLAY

The READER asks each WRITER in turn to call out a word—an adjective or a noun or whatever the space calls for—and uses them to fill in the blank spaces in the joke. The result is a MAD LIBS® game.

When the READER then reads the completed MAD LIBS® game to the other players, they will discover that they have told a fantastic, screamingly funny, shocking, silly, crazy, or just plain dumb joke—depending upon which words each WRITER called out.

• EXAMPLE (*Before* and *After*)

What did the policeman say when he gave the bus driver

a/an ______________ for ____________________ through a red light?
NOUN VERB ENDING IN "ING"

"You just got *bus*-ted!"

What did the policeman say when he gave the bus driver

a CACTUS for SWIMMING through a red light?
NOUN VERB ENDING IN "ING"

"You just got *bus*-ted!"

MAD LIBS®

QUICK REVIEW

In case you have forgotten what adjectives, adverbs, nouns, and verbs are, here is a quick review:

An ADJECTIVE describes something or somebody. *Lumpy, soft, ugly, messy,* and *short* are adjectives.

An ADVERB tells how something is done. It modifies a verb and usually ends in "ly." *Modestly, stupidly, greedily,* and *carefully* are adverbs.

A NOUN is the name of a person, place, or thing. *Sidewalk, umbrella, bridle, bathtub,* and *nose* are nouns.

A VERB is an action word. *Run, pitch, jump,* and *swim* are verbs. Put the verbs in past tense if the directions say PAST TENSE. *Ran, pitched, jumped,* and *swam* are verbs in the past tense.

When we ask for A PLACE, we mean any sort of place: a country or city *(Spain, Cleveland)* or a room *(bathroom, kitchen).*

An EXCLAMATION or SILLY WORD is any sort of funny sound, gasp, grunt, or outcry, like *Wow!, Ouch!, Whomp!, Ick!,* and *Gadzooks!*

When we ask for specific words, like a NUMBER, a COLOR, an ANIMAL, or a PART OF THE BODY, we mean a word that is one of those things, like *seven, blue, horse,* or *head.*

When we ask for a PLURAL, it means more than one. For example, *cat* pluralized is *cats.*

MAD LIBS® is fun to play with friends, but you can also play it by yourself! To begin with, DO NOT look at the jokes on the page below. Fill in the blanks on this page with the words called for. Then, using the words you have selected, fill in the blank spaces in the jokes.

Now you've created your own hilarious MAD LIBS® game!

ADJECTIVE ______________________

ANIMAL ______________________

NOUN ______________________

PERSON IN ROOM ______________________

ADJECTIVE ______________________

A PLACE ______________________

PART OF THE BODY ______________________

COLOR ______________________

Rick: Knock! Knock!

Morty: Who's there?

Rick: Eat Mop.

Morty: Eat Mop who?

Rick: You want me to *eat your poo*? You're a/an __________ (ADJECTIVE) little __________ (ANIMAL), Morty.

Why did Robot Rick blow a/an __________ (NOUN)?

__________ (PERSON IN ROOM) wouldn't stop *pressing his buttons*.

Why couldn't Birdperson's __________ (ADJECTIVE) family make it to (the) __________ (A PLACE)?

They were under the *feather*.

What advice did Dr. Glip Glop give when his patient's __________ (PART OF THE BODY) turned __________ (COLOR)?

"Stop making *rash* decisions!"

MAD LIBS® is fun to play with friends, but you can also play it by yourself! To begin with, DO NOT look at the jokes on the page below. Fill in the blanks on this page with the words called for. Then, using the words you have selected, fill in the blank spaces in the jokes.

Now you've created your own hilarious MAD LIBS® game!

PART OF THE BODY ____________________

NOUN ____________________

TYPE OF LIQUID ____________________

ADJECTIVE ____________________

NOUN ____________________

ADJECTIVE ____________________

ANIMAL ____________________

NOUN ____________________

VERB ____________________

Why did Bill the Dog keep scratching his ______________ (PART OF THE BODY)?

Those pesky fleas kept *bugging the* ______________ (NOUN) out of him!

Rick: Knock! Knock!

Morty: Who's there?

Rick: Anita.

Morty: Anita who?

Rick: *A-nit-a* drink, Morty! Get me a/an ______________ (TYPE OF LIQUID) right now, you ______________ (ADJECTIVE) little ______________ (NOUN).

How do you know if Amish Cyborg is ______________ (ADJECTIVE) with the flu?

First, he gets a little ______________ (ANIMAL), and then he gets a little *buggy*.

What did the toilet say to the ______________ (NOUN) in Buttworld?

"You ______________ (VERB) a little *flushed*."

MAD LIBS® is fun to play with friends, but you can also play it by yourself! To begin with, DO NOT look at the jokes on the page below. Fill in the blanks on this page with the words called for. Then, using the words you have selected, fill in the blank spaces in the jokes.

Now you've created your own hilarious MAD LIBS® game!

A PLACE ____________________

VERB ____________________

NOUN ____________________

ADJECTIVE ____________________

PLURAL NOUN ____________________

NOUN ____________________

ADJECTIVE ____________________

OCCUPATION ____________________

Why did Morty take a prune to (the) ______________ (A PLACE)?

Because he couldn't ______________ (VERB) a *date*!

What do you say to Pencilvester when he wins a/an ______________ (NOUN)?

"______________ (ADJECTIVE) *point*!"

Where do Cronenbergs shop for ______________ (PLURAL NOUN)?

At the *gross*-ery ______________ (NOUN)!

What are three ______________ (ADJECTIVE) words every ______________ (OCCUPATION) dreads hearing?

"Jerry's up next."

MAD LIBS® is fun to play with friends, but you can also play it by yourself! To begin with, DO NOT look at the jokes on the page below. Fill in the blanks on this page with the words called for. Then, using the words you have selected, fill in the blank spaces in the jokes.

Now you've created your own hilarious MAD LIBS® game!

VERB ____________________

ADJECTIVE ____________________

ADJECTIVE ____________________

ANIMAL ____________________

NUMBER ____________________

OCCUPATION ____________________

PLURAL NOUN ____________________

ADJECTIVE ____________________

Why doesn't Father Bob ______________ in church?
VERB

Because he'd have to sit in his own *pew*.

Why is Morty like a/an ______________ ship at the bottom of the ocean?
ADJECTIVE

They're both ______________ *wrecks*!
ADJECTIVE

Morty: What's the difference between a/an ______________ and a fox?
ANIMAL

Rick: ______________ *drinks*.
NUMBER

Jerry: I'm here to apply for a job. I want to be a/an ______________!
OCCUPATION

I've filled out all the ______________.
PLURAL NOUN

Manager: Hmm. We've got a different opening for someone like you.

Jerry: That's ______________! What is it?
ADJECTIVE

Manager: The *door*.

MAD LIBS® is fun to play with friends, but you can also play it by yourself! To begin with, DO NOT look at the jokes on the page below. Fill in the blanks on this page with the words called for. Then, using the words you have selected, fill in the blank spaces in the jokes.

Now you've created your own hilarious MAD LIBS® game!

ADJECTIVE ________________

ADJECTIVE ________________

PLURAL NOUN ________________

OCCUPATION ________________

VERB ________________

COLOR ________________

VERB ENDING IN "ING" ________________

VERB ________________

Rick: Knock! Knock!

Morty: Who's there?

Rick: Summer.

Morty: Summer who?

Rick: *Sum-mer* ______________ (ADJECTIVE) and some are ______________ (ADJECTIVE), but they're all ______________ (PLURAL NOUN), Morty. You'll get used to it.

Jerry thought about becoming a/an ______________ (OCCUPATION) but decided there was no *future* in it.

What's Coach Feratu's favorite fruit to ______________ (VERB)?

A/An ______________ (COLOR) *orange*!

Rick: Is Mrs. Refrigerator ______________ (VERB ENDING IN "ING"), Morty?

Morty: Uh, yes.

Rick: *Then you better* ______________ (VERB) *to catch her*, Morty! Now! Before she gets away!

MAD LIBS® is fun to play with friends, but you can also play it by yourself! To begin with, DO NOT look at the jokes on the page below. Fill in the blanks on this page with the words called for. Then, using the words you have selected, fill in the blank spaces in the jokes.

Now you've created your own hilarious MAD LIBS® game!

NOUN ____________

ADJECTIVE ____________

VERB ____________

VERB ENDING IN "ING" ____________

NOUN ____________

NOUN ____________

PLURAL NOUN ____________

ANIMAL ____________

ADJECTIVE ____________

Why is Ghost in a/an __________ (NOUN) the most __________ (ADJECTIVE) liar in the universe?

Because you can __________ (VERB) *right through him.*

Did you hear about the Cat Person who had trouble __________ (VERB ENDING IN "ING") a movie on his DVD player?

Turns out he just had the __________ (NOUN) on *paws.*

What did Revolio Clockberg Jr. say when he couldn't get his __________ (NOUN) fixed?

"That really *grinds my* __________ (PLURAL NOUN)!"

Rick: I once had a/an __________ (ANIMAL) that didn't have a nose, Morty.

Morty: Oh yeah? How did it smell?

Rick: __________ (ADJECTIVE).

MAD LIBS® is fun to play with friends, but you can also play it by yourself! To begin with, DO NOT look at the jokes on the page below. Fill in the blanks on this page with the words called for. Then, using the words you have selected, fill in the blank spaces in the jokes.

Now you've created your own hilarious MAD LIBS® game!

ANIMAL ____________________

PLURAL NOUN ____________________

NOUN ____________________

NOUN ____________________

VERB ____________________

VERB ____________________

PART OF THE BODY ____________________

A PLACE ____________________

PLURAL NOUN ____________________

NUMBER ____________________

Why did Snuffles and his ______________ (ANIMAL) army transport themselves to another universe?

Because ______________ (PLURAL NOUN) on our planet were way too *ruff*.

What kind of ______________ (NOUN) does Frankenstein drive?

A *monster* ______________ (NOUN).

Morty: Knock! ______________ (VERB)!

Rick: Who's there?

Morty: Dewey.

Rick: Dewey who?

Morty: *Dew-ey* really have to ______________ (VERB) again, Rick? My ______________ (PART OF THE BODY) is tired and I want to go back to (the) ______________ (A PLACE).

What's the difference between a pile of ______________ (PLURAL NOUN) and Jerry?

One is at least worth ______________ (NUMBER) cents. *Jerry is totally worthless.*

MAD LIBS® is fun to play with friends, but you can also play it by yourself! To begin with, DO NOT look at the jokes on the page below. Fill in the blanks on this page with the words called for. Then, using the words you have selected, fill in the blank spaces in the jokes.

Now you've created your own hilarious MAD LIBS® game!

ADJECTIVE ____________________

NOUN ____________________

A PLACE ____________________

VERB ____________________

SAME VERB ____________________

PART OF THE BODY ____________________

ADJECTIVE ____________________

NOUN ____________________

Did you hear about the Courier Flap who only dated perky,

________________ men?
ADJECTIVE

It preferred *outgoing male*.

What did the Szechuan ________________ say to his date at
NOUN

the ________________ party?
A PLACE

"Want to go for a *dip*?"

Lizard Morty: ________________! ________________!
VERB / SAME VERB

Morty: Who's there?

Lizard Morty: Iguana.

Morty: Iguana who?

Lizard Morty: *I-guana* shed my skin!

My ________________ is aching.
PART OF THE BODY

How do you get Photography Raptor to take

a/an ________________ ________________?
ADJECTIVE / NOUN

Tell him he needs to *focus*!

MAD LIBS® is fun to play with friends, but you can also play it by yourself! To begin with, DO NOT look at the jokes on the page below. Fill in the blanks on this page with the words called for. Then, using the words you have selected, fill in the blank spaces in the jokes.

Now you've created your own hilarious MAD LIBS® game!

A PLACE ______________________

PERSON IN ROOM ______________________

VERB ENDING IN "ING" ______________________

PART OF THE BODY ______________________

ADJECTIVE ______________________

VERB ______________________

OCCUPATION ______________________

NOUN ______________________

A PLACE ______________________

Why did Birdperson run out of (the) ____________ (A PLACE) when the server came over?

He had a huge *bill.*

How did ________________ (PERSON IN ROOM) know that Amish Cyborg was an alcoholic?

He kept __________________ (VERB ENDING IN "ING") *off the wagon.*

Rick: Knock! Knock!

Morty: Who's there?

Rick: Kenya.

Morty: Kenya who?

Rick: *Ken-ya* close your ________________ (PART OF THE BODY) for one ______________ (ADJECTIVE) second? I'm trying to ______________ (VERB), Morty.

Jerry: Beth left me! She's gone! My ______________ (OCCUPATION), the ______________ (NOUN) of my dreams, went to (the) ______________ (A PLACE) and she's never coming back because of all my insecurities!

Beth: Take it easy, Jerry. *I was in the bathroom.*

MAD LIBS® is fun to play with friends, but you can also play it by yourself! To begin with, DO NOT look at the jokes on the page below. Fill in the blanks on this page with the words called for. Then, using the words you have selected, fill in the blank spaces in the jokes.

Now you've created your own hilarious MAD LIBS® game!

A PLACE ____________________

ADJECTIVE ____________________

TYPE OF FOOD ____________________

ADJECTIVE ____________________

PLURAL NOUN ____________________

ADJECTIVE ____________________

VERB ENDING IN "ING" ____________________

PLURAL NOUN ____________________

ADJECTIVE ____________________

Rick: Knock! Knock!

Morty: Who's there?

Rick: Dew Knot.

Morty: Dew Knot who?

Rick: *Dew Knot* go in (the) __________ (A PLACE), Morty. I took a/an __________ (ADJECTIVE) dump in there. Must've been some bad __________ (TYPE OF FOOD).

Scary Terry is so __________ (ADJECTIVE), even *blind* __________ (PLURAL NOUN) *are afraid of him.*

Did you hear the one about the __________ (ADJECTIVE) robot that was arrested for __________ (VERB ENDING IN "ING") a bunch of __________ (PLURAL NOUN)? The judge charged him with *battery*.

Why couldn't anyone find Birdperson at the __________ (ADJECTIVE) party? Because he was in *da-skies*!

MAD LIBS® is fun to play with friends, but you can also play it by yourself! To begin with, DO NOT look at the jokes on the page below. Fill in the blanks on this page with the words called for. Then, using the words you have selected, fill in the blank spaces in the jokes.

Now you've created your own hilarious MAD LIBS® game!

VERB ____________________

PART OF THE BODY (PLURAL) ____________________

VERB ____________________

VERB ____________________

ADJECTIVE ____________________

NOUN ____________________

ARTICLE OF CLOTHING (PLURAL) ____________________

ADJECTIVE ____________________

Did you ____________ the story about the single Meeseeks?
VERB

He wanted to be left *a-clone*.

Rick: Knock! Knock!

Morty: Who's there?

Rick: Dozer.

Morty: Dozer who?

Rick: *Doz-er* some big ____________________,
PART OF THE BODY (PLURAL)

aren't they, Morty? The kind I'd like to ______________.
VERB

What did Rick ____________ when he finally arrived at Ruben's
VERB

______________ sphincter?
ADJECTIVE

"This ______________ is a *dump*!"
NOUN

Why did Rick poop in his _________________________?
ARTICLE OF CLOTHING (PLURAL)

It was the ______________ thing to *doo-doo*.
ADJECTIVE

MAD LIBS® is fun to play with friends, but you can also play it by yourself! To begin with, DO NOT look at the jokes on the page below. Fill in the blanks on this page with the words called for. Then, using the words you have selected, fill in the blank spaces in the jokes.

Now you've created your own hilarious MAD LIBS® game!

VERB ENDING IN "ING" ____________________

ADVERB ____________________

PART OF THE BODY (PLURAL) ____________________

VERB ____________________

SAME VERB ____________________

ADJECTIVE ____________________

NOUN ____________________

PLURAL NOUN ____________________

OCCUPATION ____________________

How did Jerry end up ______________ (VERB ENDING IN "ING") two of his favorite balls?

He ______________ (ADVERB) stepped on a rake.

How do you know if a zombie is tired?

It's *dead* on its ______________ (PART OF THE BODY (PLURAL))!

Rick: ______________ (VERB)! ______________ (SAME VERB)!

Morty: Who's there?

Rick: M'right.

Morty: M'right who?

Rick: *M'-right* foot itches like crazy, Morty. Never wrestle a/an ______________ (ADJECTIVE) ______________ (NOUN). It will make your ______________ (PLURAL NOUN) itch. Trust me.

A rabbi, Father Bob, and a/an ______________ (OCCUPATION) walk into a bar. The bartender looks up and says, "What is this, a *joke*?"

MAD LIBS® is fun to play with friends, but you can also play it by yourself! To begin with, DO NOT look at the jokes on the page below. Fill in the blanks on this page with the words called for. Then, using the words you have selected, fill in the blank spaces in the jokes.

Now you've created your own hilarious MAD LIBS® game!

PERSON IN ROOM ______________________

ADJECTIVE ______________________

PART OF THE BODY ______________________

PERSON IN ROOM ______________________

PART OF THE BODY (PLURAL) ______________________

NOUN ______________________

ADJECTIVE ______________________

ADJECTIVE ______________________

When Beth married ____________________ (PERSON IN ROOM),

it was a very ________________ (ADJECTIVE) day.

Even the cake was in *tiers*!

What does Rick think about the difference between love and marriage?

Love is blind and marriage is a real ____________________ (PART OF THE BODY) *-opener*!

Rick: Hey, Morty. When ____________________ (PERSON IN ROOM) and your mom were first dating, he came to me on his hands and ________________________ (PART OF THE BODY (PLURAL)) and said, "Can I marry your daughter?" I said, "With what ________________ (NOUN)? You can't even afford to pay for my daughter's toilet paper!"

He said, "She told me I didn't need money for that!"

Morty: Sounds like she's *full of crap*.

Rick: I know a/an ________________ (ADJECTIVE) dumbass who sounds exactly like a/an ________________ (ADJECTIVE) owl.

Morty: *Who?!*

MAD LIBS® is fun to play with friends, but you can also play it by yourself! To begin with, DO NOT look at the jokes on the page below. Fill in the blanks on this page with the words called for. Then, using the words you have selected, fill in the blank spaces in the jokes.

Now you've created your own hilarious MAD LIBS® game!

ADJECTIVE ____________________

NOUN ____________________

PART OF THE BODY (PLURAL) ____________________

NUMBER ____________________

NOUN ____________________

ADJECTIVE ____________________

A PLACE ____________________

ADJECTIVE ____________________

What is Hamurai's ______________ fighting move?
ADJECTIVE

The ______________ *-chop*!
NOUN

Morty: Knock! Knock!

Rick: Who's there?

Morty: Ivana Seymour.

Rick: Ivana Seymour who?

Morty: *I-vana Sey-mour* ____________________! I'm a/an
PART OF THE BODY (PLURAL)

______________ -year-old ______________. It's all I think about.
NUMBER NOUN

Who did Frankenstein take to the ______________ dance?
ADJECTIVE

His *ghoul-friend*!

Why was Simple Rick crying all night in (the) ______________?
A PLACE

Because the ______________ Ricks went *a-wafer* a very long time.
ADJECTIVE

MAD LIBS® is fun to play with friends, but you can also play it by yourself! To begin with, DO NOT look at the jokes on the page below. Fill in the blanks on this page with the words called for. Then, using the words you have selected, fill in the blank spaces in the jokes.

Now you've created your own hilarious MAD LIBS® game!

OCCUPATION ______________________

NOUN ______________________

A PLACE ______________________

NOUN ______________________

VERB ______________________

PART OF THE BODY ______________________

A PLACE ______________________

NOUN ______________________

Why couldn't a/an ______________ (OCCUPATION) Morty save Hippie Morty's life when his ______________ (NOUN) capsized?

Because he was too *far out, man.*

Rick: I hear those bigwigs in (the) ______________ (A PLACE) are making a/an ______________ (NOUN) Fondlers movie. I read the script but it didn't *grab me.*

Rick: Knock! ______________ (VERB)!

Morty: Who's there?

Rick: Pullonda.

Morty: Pullonda who?

Rick: *Pull-on-da* ______________ (PART OF THE BODY) any more than you already do, Morty, and you'll end up in (the) ______________ (A PLACE).

Did you hear Jerry isn't allowed to join Beth's ______________ (NOUN) dedicated to her sentient switchblade?

He just couldn't *make the cut.*

MAD LIBS® is fun to play with friends, but you can also play it by yourself! To begin with, DO NOT look at the jokes on the page below. Fill in the blanks on this page with the words called for. Then, using the words you have selected, fill in the blank spaces in the jokes.

Now you've created your own hilarious MAD LIBS® game!

PLURAL NOUN ______________________
ADJECTIVE ______________________
NOUN ______________________
OCCUPATION ______________________
PLURAL NOUN ______________________
TYPE OF FOOD ______________________
PART OF THE BODY ______________________
VERB ENDING IN "ING" ______________________

Rick: Knock! Knock!

Morty: Who's there?

Rick: Bofah Deez.

Morty: Bofah Deez who?

Rick: *Bof-ah Deez* ______________ (PLURAL NOUN)! It's a/an ______________ (ADJECTIVE) joke, Morty. Anyone who doesn't laugh is a/an ______________ (NOUN).

Who did Baby Legs, the ______________ (OCCUPATION) with baby-sized legs, call when he fell down the ______________ (PLURAL NOUN)? The *wahhh*-mbulance!

What is Gazorpazorpfield's favorite type of ______________ (TYPE OF FOOD)? The kind that's *right in front of his* ______________ (PART OF THE BODY).

Morty: Why does Snuffles keep chasing his tail?

Rick: He's desperately ______________ (VERB ENDING IN "ING") to *make ends meet.*

MAD LIBS® is fun to play with friends, but you can also play it by yourself! To begin with, DO NOT look at the jokes on the page below. Fill in the blanks on this page with the words called for. Then, using the words you have selected, fill in the blank spaces in the jokes.

Now you've created your own hilarious MAD LIBS® game!

VERB ENDING IN "ING"	________________
PLURAL NOUN	________________
ADJECTIVE	________________
TYPE OF FOOD	________________
NOUN	________________
ADJECTIVE	________________
ADJECTIVE	________________
PLURAL NOUN	________________

Did you hear Pickle Rick is ______________ stand-up comedy?
VERB ENDING IN "ING"

He really gets off on *gherkin* people's ______________.
PLURAL NOUN

How did the Thickburger propose to the ______________ fry?
ADJECTIVE

With a/an ______________ *ring*.
TYPE OF FOOD

What did the ______________ that eats poop say when asked why he does what he does?
NOUN

"It's a/an ______________ job but somebody's gotta *doo-doo* it!"
ADJECTIVE

Rick: I heard the DJ at this year's Flu Season Dance was ______________.
ADJECTIVE

Morty: I wouldn't say that. He had some *sick* ______________.
PLURAL NOUN

MAD LIBS® is fun to play with friends, but you can also play it by yourself! To begin with, DO NOT look at the jokes on the page below. Fill in the blanks on this page with the words called for. Then, using the words you have selected, fill in the blank spaces in the jokes.

Now you've created your own hilarious MAD LIBS® game!

ADJECTIVE ________________

PLURAL NOUN ________________

PART OF THE BODY ________________

NOUN ________________

ADJECTIVE ________________

VERB ENDING IN "ING" ________________

ADJECTIVE ________________

ADJECTIVE ________________

Rick: Alcohol is the ______________ (ADJECTIVE) solvent, Morty.

Morty: Why is that, Rick?

Rick: It *dissolves* marriages, ______________ (PLURAL NOUN), careers, and anything else that gets in the way of success.

Rick: What do you call a/an ______________ (PART OF THE BODY) that's too puffy, Morty? I'll tell you: *Not worth a single* ______________ (NOUN) *of your precious time!*

Why did Morty make so many ______________ (ADJECTIVE) squirrels start ______________ (VERB ENDING IN "ING") with fear? He couldn't help it. He makes everybody *nuts*.

Morty: Rick, it's pretty ______________ (ADJECTIVE) that Fart has telepathic abilities.

Rick: That's why they call him *silent but* ______________ (ADJECTIVE), Morty.

MAD LIBS® is fun to play with friends, but you can also play it by yourself! To begin with, DO NOT look at the jokes on the page below. Fill in the blanks on this page with the words called for. Then, using the words you have selected, fill in the blank spaces in the jokes.

Now you've created your own hilarious MAD LIBS® game!

A PLACE ____________________

TYPE OF FOOD (PLURAL) ____________________

NOUN ____________________

ANIMAL ____________________

ADJECTIVE ____________________

TYPE OF FOOD (PLURAL) ____________________

A PLACE ____________________

Morty: What's the name of that thing in (the) ____________ (A PLACE) that peels potatoes, carrots, and ____________ (TYPE OF FOOD (PLURAL))?

Rick: You mean your ____________ (NOUN)? That's a *spouse*, Morty.

Rick: Hey, Morty. What do you get from a/an ____________ (ANIMAL)?

Morty: Bacon.

Rick: Very good. What do you get from a chicken?

Morty: Eggs and meat.

Rick: You know what you get from a big, ____________ (ADJECTIVE) cow? I'll tell you, Morty: *Homework*.

Rick: Knock! Knock!

Morty: Who's there?

Rick: Justin.

Morty: Justin who?

Rick: *Just-in* time to help me hide the ____________ (TYPE OF FOOD (PLURAL)). Gazorpazorpfield is in (the) ____________ (A PLACE)!

MAD LIBS® is fun to play with friends, but you can also play it by yourself! To begin with, DO NOT look at the jokes on the page below. Fill in the blanks on this page with the words called for. Then, using the words you have selected, fill in the blank spaces in the jokes.

Now you've created your own hilarious MAD LIBS® game!

PART OF THE BODY ____________

NOUN ____________

ADVERB ____________

PART OF THE BODY ____________

ARTICLE OF CLOTHING (PLURAL) ____________

NUMBER ____________

CELEBRITY ____________

PLURAL NOUN ____________

ADJECTIVE ____________

PART OF THE BODY (PLURAL) ____________

Morty: Hey, Rick, why can't my ______________ (PART OF THE BODY) be twelve inches long?

Rick: Because then it would be a *foot*, Morty.

What was Butter Robot's ______________ (NOUN) after he ______________ (ADVERB) passed the butter?

He received a *pat* on the ______________ (PART OF THE BODY).

Why were King Flippy Nips' ______________ (ARTICLE OF CLOTHING (PLURAL)) always so wet?

Because he *reigned* for ______________ (NUMBER) years.

Why did ______________ (CELEBRITY) agree to have a theme park filled with ______________ (PLURAL NOUN) placed inside his body?

It *amuse*d him.

Morty: Hey, Rick, have you heard about that ______________ (ADJECTIVE) procedure where they remove your spine and ______________ (PART OF THE BODY (PLURAL))?

Rick: Of course I have. It's called *marriage*.

MAD LIBS® is fun to play with friends, but you can also play it by yourself! To begin with, DO NOT look at the jokes on the page below. Fill in the blanks on this page with the words called for. Then, using the words you have selected, fill in the blank spaces in the jokes.

Now you've created your own hilarious MAD LIBS® game!

ADJECTIVE ____________________

NOUN ____________________

PERSON IN ROOM ____________________

PLURAL NOUN ____________________

ADJECTIVE ____________________

NOUN ____________________

ADJECTIVE ____________________

PART OF THE BODY (PLURAL) ____________________

Scary Terry is so ______________ (ADJECTIVE), when he threw a/an ______________ (NOUN), *it wouldn't come back*!

What's the difference between the ______________ (PERSON IN ROOM) Herpson Herpsons football team and a dollar bill?

You can still get *four* ______________ (PLURAL NOUN) out of a dollar bill.

Morty: Hey, Lizard Morty, did you hear about the ______________ (ADJECTIVE) chameleon that couldn't change color?

Lizard Morty: Oh yeah. Everyone knows that ______________ (NOUN). He had *a reptile* dysfunction.

Rick: Knock! Knock!

Morty: Who's there?

Rick: All kinds of ______________ (ADJECTIVE) alien ______________ (PART OF THE BODY (PLURAL)).

Morty: I don't get it, Rick.

Rick: Yeah, and *you never will*, Morty. You never will.